北京風景名勝
GREAT SITES OF BEIJING

北京工艺美术出版社　BEIJING ARTS AND CRAFTS PUBLISHING HOUSE

Great Sites of Beijing

Edited by Yuchen
Translated by Zongren
Published by Beijing Arts and Crafts Publishing House
Printed in China
First edition: 1999
ISBN 7-80526-284-5/J · 117
05000

目 录　CONTENTS

北 京 漫 话

A Glimpse of Beijing's History

中华人民共和国的首都——北京，是世界著名的历史文化名城。

1929年，考古学家在北京周口店龙骨山洞发现了第一个完整的"北京猿人"头骨化石，经研究证实，北京地区历经旧石器时代和新石器时代，这里曾经是人类文明的发祥地之一。

北京城起源于商代（约前17世纪初—约前11世纪）后期，那时这里有燕和蓟两个自然形成的方国。公元前1045年，周灭商，分封诸侯，周武王封帝尧之后于蓟，封召公奭于燕，北京始为方国之都。三千年来，尽管朝代屡屡更迭，城名也多次更换，但北京一直是中国北方的军事重镇和贸易中心，在其发展过程中，由偏居一隅的封国都城，跃居为几代名声赫赫的帝都。

北京地处华北平原北端，西、北、东三面环山，东南为平原。地理学家把这块平原形象地称为"北京湾"。古人曾以"北枕居庸，西崎太行，东连山海，南俯中原"来说明北京地理位置的重要。

公元10世纪上半叶，崛起于中国东北方的少数民族契丹族兵强马壮，越过拱卫在北京湾三面的莽莽群山，举兵南下，进入华北北部，攻占了蓟城，并把它定为辽（907—1125）的陪都，因为蓟位于它所辖区域的南部，所以改称南京，又称燕京。一个多世纪以后，中国东北方的另一个少数民族女真族起兵灭辽，建立了金，并于1153年迁都燕京，改称中都。女真族在燕京整整统治了100年，后因受到新兴蒙古族的进攻，被迫迁都汴京（今河南开封），随后蒙古族铁骑入占中都。1267年蒙古族首领忽必烈下令在中都东北郊筑建新城，4年后这位首领即在兴建中的都城内登上皇帝宝座。又过了15年，新城全部建成，这就是意大利旅行家马可·波罗在他游记中称之为"世界莫与能比"的元大都。从此，北京取代了长安、洛阳、汴梁等古都的地位，成为中国的政治、经济、军事、文化中心，并延至明（1368—1644）、清（1616—1911）两代。

公元1368年，朱元璋借助农民起义军的力量，推翻了元帝国，建立了明王朝，以应天（今江苏南京）为京师。朱元璋做了30年皇帝，死后，其孙朱允炆继位，史称建文帝。可惜好景不长，新帝的叔父燕王朱棣在自已的封地北平府起兵，发动"靖难之役"，经过三年的酷烈战争，于1402年攻入应天，夺取了帝位，翌年改元永乐，并诏"以北平为北京"，决定迁都北京。从此，全国各地的能工巧匠云集北京，开始营建城垣、宫殿、坛庙和苑囿，工程浩大，其规模远远超过了元大都。至1421年，主要工程基本完工,朱棣正式迁都北京。

　　明代的北京城参照应天南京城的规制而建,分宫城、内城和外城四重,整座城池方方正正。城的四周建有高大坚固的砖墙,四面对称地洞开16个拱形门,门洞上的城楼飞檐凌空。立于城楼,可以远眺数十里。在城的中央,至今仍保存完好的紫禁城是它的心脏。紫禁城的周围是整齐如畦、经纬分明的街巷,两旁排列着商铺、民居。弯曲的河流,美丽的苑囿,庄严神幻的古代祭坛和寺庙,戒备森严、建筑豪华的署衙官宅,错落其间,方直中融入环曲,对称中显现变化。这座具有恢宏气势和浓郁的东方色彩的古城,标志着中国的古代文明又进入到一个新的辉煌时期。

　　明朝的统治延续了270多年。1644年李自成领导的农民军打进北京城,皇帝朱由检走投无路,吊死在紫禁城后的煤山。同年,清世祖爱新觉罗·福临进关,入主北京,建立了清王朝。同历代王朝一样,新朝皇帝总要对他居住的京城大兴土木。由于民族歧视的缘故,清代实行旗、民分城居住的制度。八旗官兵及其家属圈占内城民宅,原来的居民一律搬至外城居住,北京城因此不得不增建官邸,扩充民房。1645年清皇室重建紫禁城的太和、中和、保和三大殿;1651年重修承天门,竣工后,改称天安门。其间,还开发和拓展了"三海"(南海、中海、北海)皇家园林。到了18世纪中叶,清代兴修园林之风大盛,仅在京城西北郊扩建和新建的大型园林就有5座。与此同时,信佛奉道流行,修庙造塔、建寺筑观成为时尚。据《乾隆京城全图》标绘,北京城有胡同1400余条,寺庙竟有1300余座。那时的北京城馆阁连绵,殿宇栉比,牌匾相望;市面店铺林立,商贾云集。清代国势达到极盛,成为亚洲最强大的国家。

　　遗憾的是,1840年以后,清朝国势日衰,特别是在1860年第二次鸦片战争时期,英法联军攻入北京,许多宫殿和著名的"三山五园"被联军放火烧毁,无数珍宝被劫掠到异国他乡。如今要重睹旧时北京的全部风貌和这里曾经出现过的某些波澜壮阔的历史场景已不可能。然而,当人们置身于它的城区或郊野,面对那些触目皆是的历史遗迹,却会使你感到过去的事物仿佛又回到了眼前。一座巍峨耸立的古塔,常常凝聚着一代匠人的艺术精华;一块风蚀斑驳的碑石,或许记载着一件轰动一时的壮举;一片荒草丛生、瓦砾狼藉的宫苑废址,往往引发人们无限的忧思。当人们走进紫禁城太和殿的时候,不能不联想到皇帝的金冠龙袍和奢靡无度;当人们登上万里长城的时候,眼前似乎浮现出"烽火连天远,铁骑鏖战急"的厮杀场景;当人们在颐和园昆明湖荡舟的时候,会情不自禁地体味到"若道湖光宛似镜,阿谁不是镜中人"的佳境…… 北京是一座宏大的历史博物馆,北京是一座巨大的游乐园。

　　我们从北京众多风景名胜中精选10景编辑成册,以飨读者。本书是北京悠久历史和美丽风姿的缩影,亦可作导游手册。愿朋友们喜欢它。

Beijing, capital of the People's Republic of China, is a famous historical and cultural city. In 1929 archaeologists discovered the fossil of a complete skull of a Peking Man in a cave in the Longgu Mountain, Zhoukoudian, Beijing. Study confirmed that Peking Man began to inhabit the region and lived through the Old and New Stone Ages and Beijing is one of the cradles of old civilisations.

Two dukedoms, Yan and Ji, were established and built the city of Ji during the late Shang Dynasty (c. 17th–11th century B.C.). The city was situated very close to the present city of Beijing. In 1045 B.C. the Zhou Dynasty (c. 11th century–256 B.C.) overthrew the Shang Dynasty and bestowed the land of Ji to a descendent of King Yao and the land of Yan to Shi, Duke of Zhao. The name of the city of Ji changed many times over 3,000 years, but it remained a strategic point and a trade centre and kept growing in size. It was made national capital for several dynasties.

Beijing lies at the northern tip of the North China Plains. To its west, north and east are mountain ranges; to its southeast is flat land. Geographers call the Beijing area "Beijing Bay". An ancient book describes Beijing as such:"Its head rests on the Juyong Pass; the Taihang Mountains rise to its west; to its east are mountains and the sea; and it overlooks a plain to its south."

In the early 10th century Qidan, a nomadic tribe in northeast China, grew strong, marched over the mountains into the north part of the North China Plains, took the city of Ji and made it secondary capital of the Liao Dynasty (907–1125). Because Ji was located in the southern part of their territory, the Qidan called it Nanjing, or South Capital, and also Yanjing. One century later, another tribe named Nüzhen overthrew the Liao Dynasty and established the Jin Dynasty (1115 – 1234). In 1153 they moved their capital to Yanjing and changed its name to Zhongdu. After another century, the Nüzhen were forced out of Zhongdu by the emerging power of Mongols and moved their capital to Bianjing (present–day Kaifeng in Henan Province). In 1267 Kublai Khan, chief of the Mongols, issued an order to build a new city to the northeast of the old city of Zhongdu. Kublai Khan ascended the throne in the new city four years later. But the new city was not totally completed in another 15 years. The new city was named Dadu, capital of the Yuan Dynasty, described by Marco Polo as a city "unmatchable in the world" Since then Beijing replaced Chang'an, Luoyang, Bianliang and other cities as the national capital and became the political, economic, military and cultural centre of China through the Yuan (1206 – 1368), Ming (1368 – 1644) and Qing (1644 – 1911) dynasties.

In 1368 Zhu Yuanzhang led a peasant uprising to overthrow the Yuan Dynasty and founded the Ming Dynasty. He set his capital in Yingtian (present–day Nanjing in Jiangsu Province). He stayed on the throne for 30 years and was succeeded by his grandson Zhu Yunwen (Emperor Wen Di). Zhu Di, Duke of Yan, a son of Zhu Yuanzhang, launched a war to usurp the power from his nephew, the new emperor. After three years of bloody wars, his troops occupied Yingtian in 1402. Zhu Di became Emperor Yong Le and moved the national capital from Yingtian to his base in Beijing. He summoned craftsmen from all over the country to renovate the city wall and the imperial palace and build temples and gardens. The size of the city was greatly enlarged. By 1421 main projects had been completed and Zhu Di formally established his capital in Beijing.

The city of Beijing was a copy of the city of Nanjing. It was divided into four squares one inside another: the Imperial Palace, Imperial City, Inner City and Outer City. Sixteen gates in a symmetrical pattern were located on the four sides of the Inner City. Standing on an imposing city gate tower one could see as far as several dozen kilometres away. The Imperial Palace, also known as Forbidden City, was located in the centre of Beijing. Spreading from it in a neat pattern were streets flanked with stores and residential houses. Streams flew through lakes and gardens. Temples and official mansions had majestic buildings.

The Ming Dynasty lasted for 270 years. In 1644 Li Zicheng and his peasant rebels entered Beijing. Zhu Youjian, the last emperor of the Ming Dynasty, hanged himself on a hill behind the Imperial Palace. In the same year, Aisin Gioro Fu Lin, the chief of the Manchus, came to Beijing from north of the Great Wall, chased away Li Zicheng, and founded the Qing Dynasty. As earlier emperors, he carried out a large scale renovation of the city. The troops of the Manchu Eight Banners were allowed to take any houses they liked in the Inner City. The original residents were forced to move to the Outer City. Many grand mansions were built to accommodate the new rulers. In 1645 the imperial court began to rebuild the Taihe, Zhonghe and Baohe halls in the Imperial Palace and in 1651 to rebuild the Chengtian Gate, which, upon completion, was renamed Tiananmen, or the Gate of Heavenly Peace. During the same period, the Nanhai (South Sea), Zhonghai (Middle Sea) and Beihai (North Sea) lakes were dredged and enlarged to become imperial gardens. Construction of gardens reached its heyday in the middle of the 18th century. Five large—scale gardens were built or renovated in the northeastern suburbs. Buddhism and Taoism were developing fast during the Qing Dynasty. A great number of temples were built. A map of the capital made during Emperor Qian Long's Reign marks out 1,400 side streets in Beijing and 1,300 temples. At that time, grand towers and halls stood one after another; stores lined many streets. China became the strongest country in Asia during the 18th century.

But the Qing Dynasty declined rapidly after 1840. In 1860, during the second Opium War, British and French troops invaded Beijing and looted and burnt the imperial gardens and palaces. Numerous treasures were taken out of China.

The present Beijing offers many places of historical significance. The ancient pagodas show the high artistic skills of the Chinese; inscriptions on stone tablets record major events; the ruins of looted imperial gardens bring back sorrowful memories; and the Forbidden City tells visitors how extravagant the life of emperors had been. One may envision the battle scenes when he stands on the Great Wall. Beijing is like a giant museum of history and a great amusement garden.

We present in this picture book 10 best sights in Beijing, representatives of Beijing's beauty.

天 安 门
Tian'anmen Square

　　天安门始建于明永乐十五年（1417），称"承天门"；原为明、清两代皇城的正门。历史上曾几次被雷火焚烧，1651年重修后改称"天安门"。天安门原是皇帝颁发诏令和重大政务活动的出入之门，因此，其建筑规制甚高，五洞城门，重楼九楹；在中间门洞的前后各立汉白玉石华表一对，华表顶蹲石兽，柱身遍雕祥云腾龙，另有两对石狮前后镇守。新中国成立后，门前左右增设了观礼台，台前置花坛，每当春秋季节，这里花团锦簇，人头攒动，热闹非凡。观礼台前是原皇城的御河一金水河，河上横跨汉白玉石桥5座，桥栏上雕饰着精美的龙凤云图案。天安门城楼前是世界上最大的广场一天安门广场。

　　1949年10月1日，毛泽东主席在天安门城楼上宣告中华人民共和国成立。

　　Tian'anmen was the front gate of the Imperial Palace during the Ming and Qing dynasties. Originally built in 1417 and named Chengtianmen, it was burnt down and rebuilt several times. The present gate tower was rebuilt in 1651 and renamed Tian'anmen. Ming and Qing emperors would issue decrees from the gate tower. The gate has five openings and nine tiers of eaves. Two pairs of white marble pillars stand inside and outside the central opening. Each stone pillar has a stone beast crouching on top and carvings of clouds and a dragon around it. There are also two pairs of stone lions inside and outside the gate. After the founding of new China reviewing stands were built on the two sides of the gate. In spring and autumn flowers in front of the reviewing stands attract many visitors. Five white marble bridges span the Golden Water River which flows in front of Tian'anmen. In front of the gate is the world's largest open ground in the city — Tian'anmen Square. The late Chairman Mao Zedong proclaimed the founding of the People's Republic on the gate tower on October 1, 1949.

天安门城楼 为重楼庑殿顶，朱柱黄瓦，雄伟壮观，城楼已对公众开放，登楼远眺，更觉天安门广场宽广博大。

Gate Tower of Tian'anmen The grand city gate tower is open to the public. From it one has a whole view of Tian'anmen Square.

天安门广场　总面积44.5公顷，它的北侧为天安门，中央为人民英雄纪念碑，碑南是毛泽东主席纪念堂，东有中国历史博物馆，西有人民大会堂。广场布局严整，气势宏阔。

Tian'anmen Square　The centre of Beijing occupies 44.5 hectares. Tian'anmen stands to its north; the Monument to the People's Heroes rises in the middle; south of the monument is the Memorial Hall of Chairman Mao Zedong; and to the east is the Museum of Chinese History and to its west is the Great Hall of the People.

人民大会堂 为全国人民代表大会的会址,也是人大常委会的办公处,总面积17万多平方米。正门檐部悬挂着中华人民共和国国徽。图为从天安门城楼看人民大会堂。

Great Hall of the People The 170,000-square-meter building serves as the meeting place of the National People's Congress. It houses the offices of the Standing Committee members. The national emblem hangs above the front gate. The picture was taken from the gate tower of Tian'anmen.

故　宫
Palace Museum

　　故宫旧称紫禁城,是明、清两朝皇宫,曾有24个皇帝在这里处理朝政和居住。

　　故宫建于明永乐四年至十八年(1406—1420)。它占地72万平方米,共有房屋号称9999间半(现存8000余间),约15万平方米,是中国现存最大的皇宫。故宫的建筑布局分外朝、内廷两部分。外朝以太和、中和、保和三大殿为主体,左右衔连文华、武英两建筑群。三大殿以北为内廷,内廷又分中、东、西三路,中为乾清宫、交泰殿、坤宁宫,其后是御花园,中路两侧是东、西六宫。这种布局,充分体现了古礼所谓"前朝后寝"的格局。前朝为"大内正衙",是皇帝处理政务的地方;后寝即所谓"三宫六院",是皇后和妃嫔的居所。

　　故宫座落于北京城中轴线,整个建筑主体突出,左右对称,层次分明,体现了中国古代建筑的优秀传统和独特风格。宫内珍藏有大量文物和艺术品,是中国重点文物保护单位。

　　Known to many as the Forbidden City, the Palace Museum was the Imperial Palace of the Ming and Qing dynasties.

　　The palace was constructed from 1406 to 1420. On its ground of 720,000 square meters there are several dozen compounds of various sizes with 8,000-odd rooms (originally there were 9,999 and half rooms).The Imperial Palace is divided into the Outer Court and Inner Court. Main structures are arranged symmetrically along a central axis in a clear-cut pattern. Three main halls in the Outer Court, Hall of Supreme Harmony, Hall of Middle Harmony and Hall of Preserving Harmony were where the emperor conducted grand ceremonies. The main structures in the Inner Court are Palace of Heavenly Purity, Hall of Harmonious Union and Palace of Earthly Tranquillity. The emperor lived and handled state affairs there. The Six Eastern palaces and the Six Western Palaces on the two sides were living quarters for imperial consorts.

　　The Palace Museum is the largest and best preserved imperial building complex in China. It keeps a great number of cultural relics and master pieces of art.

故宫远眺

A Distant View of the Palace Museum

午门　为故宫正门，通高35.6米，下为砖石墩台。它居中向阳，位当子午，故称午门。门为五洞，中门供皇帝出入，叫"御路"；王公大臣走左右门；掖门平时不开，唯殿试时，文武进士按单双号进左右掖门。

Meridian Gate (Wumen) The front gate to the Imperial Palace is 35.6 meters high. Five gate towers rise majestically on a gigantic base of stone and bricks. The gate has five openings. The central one was used exclusively by the emperor. Court officials passed through the two gates near the central one. The two side-gates were opened only to let in successful candidates of imperial examinations.

内金水河 河水源于北京西郊玉泉山，从故宫西北角地沟流入宫中，河道幽幽，水清似玉，故又名玉带河。

Inner Golden Water River Fed by spring water from Yuquan Hill on the western outskirts of Beijing, the canal runs from northwestern corner and through the Imperial Palace. It is also called "Jade Belt River" for its clear water of emerald colour.

外朝三大殿　是故宫最主要的建筑群，从右至左分别为太和、中和、保和殿，这里是皇帝举行大典、召见群臣和行使权力的主要场所。

Three Main Halls in the Outer Court　The Hall of Supreme Harmony, Hall of Middle Harmony and Hall of Preserving harmony (from right to left) are the main halls in the Outer Court. They were where the emperor attended grand ceremonies and held audiences.

太和殿 俗称金銮殿，建于1420年。大殿面阔11间，进深5间，通高35.5米，总面积2300平方米。它是中国现存最大的木构殿。明、清两朝皇帝即位、大婚、朝会以及元旦赐宴、命将出征和金殿传胪等，均在此举行。

Hall of Supreme Harmony (Taihedian) Popularly known as the Gold Throne Hall, it was built in 1420. The hall is 35.5 meters high and covers an area of 2,300 square meters. Grand ceremonies such as the coronation, wedding and birthday celebration of the emperor and sending off an expedition army were held in this hall.

太和殿内景　殿内陈设如当年帝、后临朝状。正中为7级高台平床；上设屏风、宝座、御案，两侧为宫扇、珐琅塔和仙鹤。殿内金碧辉煌、庄严华贵。

Inside the Hall of Supreme Harmony　The interior of this hall is preserved as in ancient times. On the raised platform is the gilded imperial throne placed on a dais two meters high. Behind the throne is a carved screen. On either side of the throne are a crane-shaped candlestick, an elephant-shaped incense burner with a pagoda on top which are all cloisonne wares.

中和殿　位于太和殿以北，为深广各5间的方形殿，四角攒尖，鎏金宝顶。每逢大典，皇帝在此小憩，然后乘肩舆至太和殿。

Hall of Middle Harmony (Zhonghedian)　The square hall with a paramedic roof stands behind the Hall of Supreme Harmony. The emperor would take a rest before he went to the Hall of Supreme Harmony to preside grand ceremonies.

云龙石雕　嵌于保和殿后的殿基上。保和殿是外朝最后的大殿，面阔9楹，深5间，重檐垂脊，黄瓦朱柱，宏丽挺拔。云龙石雕是北京城最大的石雕艺术品，通长16.75米，宽3.07米，厚1.07米，重约250吨。石面精刻海涛山崖、流云游龙，刀法精绝，造型生动。

Dragon—Cloud Jade Carving　It is placed behind the Hall of Preserving Harmony. The largest carving in Beijing is 16.75 meters long, 3.07 meters wide and 1.07 meters thick and weighs 250 tons. On it are exquisite designs of mountain cliffs, sea waves, clouds and nine dragons.

内廷鸟瞰 内廷分中、东、西三路。图中从右至左分别为乾清宫、交泰殿和坤宁宫,其后是御花园;图中上为东六宫,下为西六宫。整体布局主体突出, 简繁得当, 虽有千门万户, 却又有条不紊。

A Bird's-eye View of the Inner Court The buildings of the Inner Court are arranged along three routes. In the picture from right to left are the Palace of Heavenly Purity, the Hall of Harmonious Union and the Palace of Earthly Tranquillity. Behind them is the Imperial Garden. The Six Western Palaces appear in the lower part of the picture and the Six Eastern Palaces appear in the upper part of the picture.

乾清宫内景　正中为宝座，座后为金漆屏风，其上悬"正大光明"横匾。清代自康熙皇帝（1662—1722在位）以后，生前不宣布皇位继承人，而是将继承人名字写好后封于密匣，放置匾后，一旦皇帝驾崩，由辅政大臣当众开匣，宣布皇帝继承人。

Inside the Palace of Heavenly Purity　The throne is placed in the middle of the hall. Above the throne is a horizontal plaque with the characters meaning "Upright and Honest". Emperor Kang Xi of the Qing Dynasty set the rule that the successor of the emperor was kept in secret. The name of the successor would be written on a piece of paper which was locked in a box and the box would be placed behind the plaque. When the emperor died the box was opened to make the successor known.

乾清宫　为内廷正殿，明、清两朝皇帝皆以此殿为寝宫，并在此处理朝政。皇帝驾崩，停棺柩于殿内。它是内廷等级最高的大殿。

Palace of Heavenly Purity（Qianqinggong）　The highest building of the Inner Court was the living quarter of the emperor during the Ming and Qing dynasties. He also did some daily work here. After his death, his bier was also laid there.

乾清宫宝座 这是整体贴金并镶嵌若干红、绿宝石的金椅，其扶手和靠背均由金龙缠绕而成；座后为金漆屏风，屏风正中镌刻着"惟天、惟圣、惟臣、惟民"八个金字，是为皇帝律己格言。

Throne in the Palace of Heavenly Purity The throne is covered with gold leafs and decorated with red and green precious stones. The handles and back are dragons woven with gold thread. On the gold-painted screen behind the throne is the emperor's motto: "Only for Heaven, the Saint, the court officials and the people."

交泰殿内景 交泰殿外形如中和殿，殿名寓示天地交泰、帝后和美。皇后逢大典或寿辰，在此殿接受妃嫔及随臣朝贺。图中宝座后及地平床两侧均为存放的宝玺，即皇帝之印，共25方，取此数大约是祈求上天保佑"大清得享二十有五之数"，然清进关后仅传十代便寿终了。

Inside the Hall of Harmonious Union (Jiaotaidian) The interior of this hall is similar to that of the Hall of Middle Harmony. Its name means "Heaven and earth are united", symbolising the harmonious relationship between the emperor and the empress. The empress received greetings from imperial concubines and attending officials on her birthday in this hall. Twenty-five imperial seals are displayed behind the throne and on a platform.

坤宁宫大婚洞房 坤宁宫在明代为皇后寝宫,清代按满族习俗改建后,殿东两间暖阁为皇帝大婚之所,殿中部为祭神场所。据史载,清康熙、同治（1862—1874在位）、光绪（1875—1908在位）三帝均在此完婚。图中喜床上用品均为原物。

Bridal Chamber After the renovation of the Palace of Earthly Tranquillity according to Manchu's customs the anteroom to the east of the Palace of Earthly Tranquillity became the bridal chamber. According to history records, weddings of emperors Kang Xi, Tong Zhi and Guang Xu were held here. The bridal chamber has preserved the same decoration as used at the wedding of Emperor Guang Xu (reigned 1875–1908).

储秀宫内景　储秀宫是西
六宫之一，慈禧太后发迹
前曾以贵人身份入住后殿，
并在此生下同治皇帝。图
中"顺时施宜"横匾为光绪
皇帝亲题，意为顺乎潮流，
百事遂愿。

Palace of Gathering Elegance
(Chuxiugong) It is one of
the Six Western Palaces.
Empress Dowager Ci Xi
moved to live here after she
was promoted to Ladyship
and gave birth to the future
Emperor Tong Zhi. The
inscription in the handwriting
of Emperor Guang Xu carved
on the plaque in the picture
means "Go along with time
and adapt to the
environment".

养心殿内景　清代自雍正皇
帝以后，除太和殿外，皇帝
均以养心殿为寝宫，并在此
处理朝政。慈禧太后揽权期
间，在此垂帘听政。图中宝
座后有一黄纱帘，慈禧太后
于帘后决定军国大事，帘前
小皇帝仅作摆设。六岁的同
治皇帝、四岁的光绪皇帝曾
先后在此充当傀儡。

Hall of Mental Cultivation
(Yangxindian) Qing
emperors after Yong Zheng
all used this hall as their
bedroom and office. After the
1861 Coup Empress Dowager
Ci Xi took over the power
and began to "hold court
behind the curtain". She
would sit behind a yellow
gauze curtain while the six-
year-old emperor Tong Zhi,
and after Tong Zhi died, the
four-year-old emperor Guang
Xu would sit in front the
curtain.

御花园 是帝后游憩之所，园中有亭台楼阁20余座，各建筑之间以五色石子甬道相连。花园精巧玲珑,典雅富丽,是中国颇具特色的宫廷花园。图为园内万春亭。

Imperial Garden The Imperial Garden was exclusively reserved for the use of the emperor and his consorts. The two dozen pavilions, towers and halls are surrounded by rockeries, flower beds and miniature landscapes. Paths are paved with pebbles in various designs. In the picture is the 10,000–Spring Pavilion. (wan chunting).

角楼 故宫宫墙四隅各设角楼一座，楼为6个歇山顶组合而成的奇特整体，3层屋檐设计有28个翼角，72条脊，造型精巧别致，为中国古代建筑艺术的杰作。

Corner Tower At each of the four corners of the Palace stands a unique tower, each with six hipped and gabled roofs. The three tiered eaves sloping into 28 upturning curves, with 72 ridges, add much grace to the structure.

天　坛
Temple of Heaven

　　天坛是明、清两代皇帝祭天、祈谷的场所，建于1406—1420年。它占地273公顷，建筑布局呈"回"字形，由两道坛墙构成内坛、外坛两大部分。主要建筑物集中在内坛南北两端的中轴线上，其间由一条宽阔的"海漫大道"—"丹陛桥"相连结，由南至北分别为圜丘坛、皇穹宇、祈年殿、皇乾殿、北天门等；中轴线以西有斋宫，以东有神厨库和宰牲亭；另有双环亭、长廊和七星石等建筑和景点。

　　明、清两代，每年农历正月十五，皇帝至祈年殿举行祈谷礼，祈祷皇天上帝保佑五谷丰登；夏至如遇旱情，至圜丘坛举行"常雩礼"，为百谷祈求膏雨；冬至则在圜丘坛举行告祀礼，向皇天上帝奏报，百谷业已丰登。若为大合祭，主祭皇天上帝，配祭皇帝的列祖列宗，以及日月星辰、云雨风雷。由此不难看出，这种隆重的典仪活动，既是帝王崇敬上天的一种礼仪，也是帝王借此显示自己至高无上，至尊至贵的一种方式。

　　天坛以其独特的设计，精绝的建筑，在世界古典建筑之林中，占有特殊的地位，从而成为著名的旅游胜地。

　　During the Ming and Qing dynasties, the emperor came to the Temple of Heaven to pray for good harvest. Its construction continued from 1406 to 1420.

　　The whole complex has an area of 273 hectares with a layout in two squares one inside the other. Two walls divide the ground into the outer and inner parts. Main structures are located on the ends of a flagstone-paved central north-south path: from south to north are the Circular Mound Altar, Imperial Vault of Heaven, Hall of Prayer for Good Harvest and Huangqian Hall. Auxiliary structures include Divine Kitchen, Slaughter Pavilion, Palace of Abstinence, Double-Circle Longevity Pavilion and Long Corridor.

　　On the 15th day of the first lunar month the emperor would come to the Hall of Prayer for Good Harvest to solicit from Heaven for good harvests. When a serious drought occurred he would pray to Heaven at the Circular Mound Altar for rain. In early winter he would come again to thank Heaven for its blessings of the year's harvest. The emperor also came to the Temple of Heaven to pay homage to his ancestors.

　　The Temple of Heaven is an outstanding representative of Chinese traditional architecture for its clever design and harmonious colours.

斋宫　位于天坛中轴线以西，整个斋宫占地约40,000平方米，共有房屋60余间，布局严谨，建筑紧凑，人称"小皇宫"。图为斋宫正殿，殿内顶部为拱券形，不露梁枋大木，俗称"无梁殿"。

Palace of Abstinence　The square compound on an area of 40,000 square meters contains 60 houses arranged in strict patterns. The picture shows the Main Hall with an arched ceiling. No beams can be seen inside, thus its another name "Beamless Hall".

天坛俯瞰

A Bird's-eye View of the Temple of Heaven

正殿内景 这里是皇帝的斋戒之所。按典制规定,皇帝在祭天前3天,必须到斋宫独宿3昼夜,其间不食荤腥、不饮酒、不娱乐、不近女色、不理刑名,这就是所谓"斋戒",以表皇帝敬天之心专一致诚。

Inside the Main Hall The emperor was supposed to fast for three days in this hall before he started the ceremony to pay homage to Heaven. During this time he abstained from meat, wine, entertainment, women and attending state affairs.

天坛晨曦

The Temple of Heaven in the Morning.

祈年殿 亦称祈谷坛，是明清两代皇帝孟春祈谷的圣殿。它是一座镏金宝顶、蓝瓦朱柱、金漆彩绘的三重檐的圆形大殿。此殿采用上屋下坛的构造形式，殿高32米，底部直径24.2米，三重檐逐层向上收缩，作伞状，耸立于高约6米、占地5900平方米的三层汉白玉石雕栏环抱的圆形台基上，大有拔地擎天之势，气势非凡，极为壮观。

Hall of Prayer for Good Harvest (Qiniandian) Also known as Qigu Hall, it was the spot where the emperor of the Ming and Qing dynasties prayed for good harvest in spring. The umbrella-like structure is 32 meters high and 24.2 meters around at the base. The six-meter-high white marble base of three tiers occupies an area of 5,900 square meters.

祈年殿雪景

Snow-covered Hall of Prayer for Good Harvest

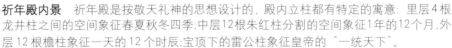

祈年殿内景　祈年殿是按敬天礼神的思想设计的，殿内立柱都有特定的寓意：里层4根龙井柱之间的空间象征春夏秋冬四季;中层12根朱红柱分割的空间象征1年的12个月,外层12根檐柱象征一天的12个时辰;宝顶下的雷公柱象征皇帝的"一统天下"。

Inside the Hall of Prayer for Good Harvest　The pillars inside the hall all have a meaning: the four in the inner circle represent the four seasons of the year; the 12 pillars in the middle circle represent 12 months of the year and the 12 pillars in the outer circle represent 12 time periods of the day. The Leigong (Thunder God) Pillar under the centre of the ceiling means the absolute power of the emperor.

皇穹宇 为单檐圆形殿宇，覆蓝色琉璃瓦，镏金宝顶，其形若伞，端庄秀丽。它是专门用来安放神牌的殿宇，俗称寝宫，高19.5米，底部直径15.6米，全木结构，殿顶由8根立柱支撑，顶无横梁，由众多斗拱上叠，天花板层层收缩，构成美丽的穹窿圆顶式藻井。皇穹宇外形挺拔舒展，观之令人赏心悦目。

Imperial Vault of Heaven (Huangqiongyu)　The circular structure has a roof covered with blue glazed tiles and topped with a gilt ball. The place was used to keep wooden tablets for worship. It is 19.5 meters high and 15.6 meters around at the base. Built entirely of wood, the vault is supported by eight pillars. The roof has no beams but only a great number of brackets entwined within each other. The ceiling tapers upward to form a beautiful caisson.

丹陛桥 是连接祈年殿和皇穹宇的南北大道，长360米，宽29.4米，因道下有一隧洞与其交叉，故名桥。桥体南端高约1米，北端高约4米，由南向北逐渐升高，象征皇帝步步登高，寓"升天"之意。由于是升天之路，所以又叫"神道"；神道两侧，左为"御道"，右为"王道"。天帝神灵走神道，皇帝走御道，王公大臣走王道。

Danbi Bridge　It is actually the main road in the Temple of Heaven between the Hall of Prayer for Good Harvest and Imperial Vault of Heaven. It is 360 meters long and 29.4 meters wide. A tunnel passes through under the road, so it is called a bridge. The southern end of the path is one meter above the ground and the northern end of it is four meters above the ground. The rise meant to "step upward toward Heaven". The cen-tral path was reserved for divine gods; the path on the left was reserved for the emperor and the path on the right was used by court officials.

皇穹宇内景 正中宝座上是皇天上帝的神位，上面为满汉文金字。皇天上帝神位两侧是皇帝先辈的神位。祭天前，皇帝至此阅览祝板，上香恭奉神位；正式祭天前，恭请各神位至祭天台。

Inside the Imperial Vault of Heaven A wooden memorial tablet of Heavenly Emperor is placed in the middle of the throne. Flanking it are tablets of the emperor's ancestors. One day before the ceremony to pray to Heaven the emperor came to this place to burn incense sticks in front of the memorial tablets.

回音壁 实为皇穹宇的圆形围墙,周长193.2米,高3.7米,厚0.9米,直径61.5米。若两人分别站在东西墙根,一人对墙低声说话,另一人可以清晰听见。这就是著名的回音壁。

Echo Wall The circular wall surrounding the Imperial Vault of Heaven is 193.2 meters long, 3.7 meters high and 0.9 meter thick. If one speaks against the wall at one end another can hear his voice at the other end of it.

圆丘坛 是一座由汉白玉石雕栏围绕的三层石造圆台,通高5米,洁白如玉,极为壮观。圆台周围砌有里圆外方的两道坛墙,表示"天圆地方"。明清两代,每年冬至皇帝亲临此坛祭天,其意为向皇天上帝奏报年丰政和,并祈求来年国泰民安。

Circular Mound Altar Also known as Heaven Mound Altar, it is five meters high and of three tiers. Around each tier there are white marble balusters. During the Ming and Qing dynasties in early winter the emperor would come to this mound to pay homage to Heaven and pray for peace and a good harvest. The mound is surrounded by two walls. The square wall represents the earth while the circular wall represents Heaven because in ancient times people believed the earth was square and Heaven round.

九龙柏 生长于回音壁墙外，相传是明永乐年间栽植的，距今500余年。因树干扭结纠缠，宛若九龙盘旋，故名九龙柏。

Nine-Dragon Cypress The tree outside the Echo Wall was planted 500 years ago. Its twining branches look like nine dragons.

太极石 即上层坛面的中心石。当人们站在此石上轻唤一声,可马上听到响亮的回音。在清代,有人说这是上天垂象的吉兆,象征皇朝固若金汤,并将这块圆石叫作"亿兆景从石"。

Taiji Stone The stone is placed in the centre of the top tier of the Circular Mound Altar. When people stand on it and shout echoes will be heard. People of the Qing Dynasty believed hearing the echoes was an auspicious omen from Heaven.

长廊 共72间,呈"W"形,是祭祀时运送祭品的廊道。原为通脊连檐,前有窗,后有墙,故又名七十二连房。

Long Corridor The corridor in the pattern of a "W" has 72 sections. It was used to deliver sacrificial objects during the ceremony to pay homage to Heaven.

双环亭　位于祈年殿西侧柏林中。公元1741年，乾隆皇帝为他母亲庆祝50大寿，在中南海修建此亭。1977年从原址迁到这里供人观赏。双环亭为两个圆亭套合而成，造型新颖，可谓木构架建筑中的奇葩。

Double-Circle Longevity Pavilion　The pavilion was originally built in 1741 by Emperor Qian Long to celebrate his mother's 50th birthday in the Imperial Palace. In 1977 it was relocated in a cypress grove on the western side of the Hall of Prayer for Good Harvest. It is a master piece of wooden structures from ancient times.

北海公园
Beihai Park

　　北海公园位于北京市中心，被誉为"世界上建园最早的皇城御园"。全园面积68.2公顷，其中水面38.9公顷。公园山青水秀，建筑华美，景色迷人，是北京著名的旅游胜地之一。

　　早在公元10世纪，辽代（907-1125）就在这里始建行宫；金代（1115-1234）则在这里挖海垒岛，用大批太湖石堆砌假山，起殿筑阁，立坊造栏，建成一座离宫。元代（1271-1368）三次扩修这里的琼华岛，并以此为中心建造大都城。明亦大兴土木，在湖滨建五龙亭。清代乾隆年间（1736-1796），这里连续施工37年，改建和兴建各式建筑200多座，至此，一座规模宏大，设计精巧的皇家园林终臻完美。

　　The park in the centre of Beijing has an area of 68.2 hectares with a water surface of 38.9 hectares. The earliest imperial garden in the world today attracts visitors with its exquisitely laid-out landscape and beautiful buildings.

　　The imperial court of the Liao Dynasty (907-1125) built a temporary palace on the site of present Beihai Park in the 10th century. During the following Jin Dynasty (1115-1234) a lake was dug. The excavated earth was piled to make a hill. Around the lake and on the hill palatial halls, corridors and pavilions were erected. The imperial court of the Yuan Dynasty (1271-1368) expanded Qionghua Islet in the lake and made it the centre of its capital Dadu City. During the Ming Dynasty five pavilions linked with zigzag bridges were built in the northwestern part of the lake. During the reign of Emperor Qian Long (1736-1796) a large-scale project was carried on over 37 years, making the place a grand imperial garden.

俯瞰北海公园　琼华岛四面临水,岛南有永安桥连接团城；岛上万木苍郁,殿阁栉比,巍巍白塔立于琼华岛之颠，成为北海公园的标志。

A Bird's—eye View of Beihai Park　The small island in Beihai Lake is connected with the Circular City by Yong'an Bridge. A giant white pagoda rises on top of it. The pagoda is the symbol of the park.

团城　为砖砌的圆形小城，位于公园南门外。城台高4.6米，周长276米，全城面积4553平方米，上有各式建筑十余座，并有古木怪石点缀其间，环境优美清雅。

Circular City (Tuancheng)　The small castle outside the southern gate of Beihai Park was built on a base of 4.6 meters high. It is surrounded by a circular wall of 276 meters long. The seclusive garden is decorated with palatial halls and pavilions and ancient trees.

承光殿　为团城主体建筑，其平面为"十"字形，前后有方形月台，正中是重檐大殿，殿四面出抱厦，顶覆黄琉璃瓦绿剪边，飞檐翘角，宏丽轩昂。明代帝后常来此观烟火，清代改为佛堂，内供白玉佛。

Chengguang Hall　The main structure in the Circular City has a square platform in front and a roof of several tiers of flying eaves. The roof is covered with glazed yellow tiles and edged with green glazed tiles. During the Ming Dynasty the emperor liked to come here to watch fireworks. It was converted into a Buddha hall during the Qing Dynasty. Now there is a Buddha statue of white jade in it.

白玉佛　用整块白玉雕凿而成,高1.5米,顶冠袈裟饰金箔,并嵌有红绿晶石。佛像肌肤洁白,色泽青润,神态祥和。1900年八国联军攻入北京,在北海抢劫珍宝时,砍坏玉佛左臂,至今刀痕犹存。

White Jade Buddha Statue　The 1.5-meter statue is carved from one piece of white jade. Its crown and cassock are ornamented with gold foils, ruby and emerald. The fair-countenance of the Buddha looks amiable. In 1900 when an allied force by eight imperialist powers looted Beijing, the left arm of the statue was cut off.

白塔 是琼华岛的主体建筑。塔南的永安寺从山门至白塔，层层递高，上下串连，构成琼华岛景区的中轴线。白塔建于 1651 年，塔高 35.9 米，下承折角式须弥座，座上为覆钵式塔身，其正面的壶形眼光门内刻藏文咒语。白塔造型挺拔轩昂，气势非凡。

White Pagoda It was originally built in 1651 but collapsed in an earthquake. The present structure was a later reconstruction. The lamaist dagoba is 35.9 meters high with a tiered base and a body like an upturned bowl. Sutras in Tibetan language are carved inside the front gate.

延楼游廊　位于琼华岛北山麓，环湖而建，上下两层，凡60间，长300米，是仿江苏镇江金山江天寺而建的观景廊。

Long Corridor　The 300-meter-long corridor of two layers runs along the shore of Beihai Lake. It is a copy of the corridor in Jiangtian Temple in Zhenjiang, Jiangsu Province.

琼华岛夜景 岛上灯火辉煌，湖中水清月满，景色迷人。古人诗赞："五亭宛宛似游龙，绿水弯环太液通，向映画船亭畔泊，藕花摇曳麝香风"。

Qionghua Islet at Night The tiny island is aflame with lights and the lake reflects a full moon. An ancient poem describes the scene: "Five pavilions shimmer on emerald water like dragons; leisure boats anchor amidst lotus flowers."

五龙亭　建于北海北岸。五亭间由白石护栏相连,远看形似游龙。在清代,这里是帝、后垂钓、观烟火和赏月的地方。

Five-Dragon Pavilions　The five waterborne pavilions are connected by zigzag bridge. The one in the middle is the largest. In old days the emperor and his consorts came here to fish, watch fireworks or admire the moon.

九龙壁 建于1756年，壁高5米，厚1.2米，长27米。整壁用彩色琉璃瓦镶砌而成，壁两面各有蟠龙9条，飞腾戏珠于海涛云气之中。九龙壁是中国琉璃建筑艺术中的上乘之作。

Nine-Dragon Screen Made in 1756, the screen wall is five meters high, 1.2 meters thick and 27 meters long. The whole thing is built with glazed colour bricks. On either side of it there are nine dragons, also made of glazed bricks, each playing with a pearl amidst waves of clouds.

画舫斋 为北海公园一处园中之园，位于湖东岸。小园的所有建筑环池而设，五楹阔殿是它的主体建筑。这里既有北方庭院浑厚持重的建筑风格，又不失江南园林柔媚细腻的点景特色。乾隆皇帝曾赞曰：〝斋似江南彩画舟，坐来轩槛镜中浮〞，特命〝画舫斋〞。

Studio of Painted Boat (Huafangzhai) It is another independent small garden in Beihai Park on the eastern shore of the lake. The main structures are arranged around a pond. Emperor Qian Long wrote a poem:"The house looks like a painted boat; and one sitting in it feels floating on water."

静心斋 位于公园北端，是北海公园又一处园中园。大园林中包含小园林是大型皇家园林的特征之一，被称为"园中园"。静心斋始建于明代，1759年扩建，园中殿堂华美，亭榭精巧，怪石争奇，小溪跌玉，游人置身园中，一步一景，其乐无穷。

Studio of Rested Heart (Jingxinzhai) During the Qing Dynasty a typical gardening feature was to build smaller gardens inside a large garden. This small garden in Beihai Park was built during the Ming Dynasty and was enlarged in 1759 during the Qing Dynasty. The palatial halls, tranquil rooms, rockeries in strange shapes and a stream provide changing sights.

小西天观音殿 位于五龙亭西北，是乾隆皇帝为其母孝圣皇太后祝寿祈福而修建的大殿，其平面为方形，四面环水，有桥可通；殿内正中设有佛教中象征"极乐世界"的须弥山。它是中国现存最大的方亭式大殿。

Guanyin Hall of Minor Western Heaven Western Heaven in Buddhism is the Land of Extreme Happiness. Emperor Qian Long built the Guanyin Hall of Minor Western Heaven to pray for his mother's happiness and longevity. It is the largest palatial hall in the style of a square pavilion in China.

颐 和 园
Summer Palace

　　颐和园位于北京市西北郊，距市中心约15公里。它是中国现存保护最完整、建筑规模最大的皇家园林和行宫。

　　颐和园原名清漪园，建成于1764年。它占地290公顷，其中水面220公顷。园内分宫廷区、前山前湖区和后山后湖区三大景区，共有殿堂楼阁、亭台水榭3000余间，是清代帝、后政治活动和游憩的地方。1860年第二次鸦片战争时，英法联军攻入北京，清漪园被焚毁。1888年慈禧太后挪用海军军费500万两白银重建，历时10年，竣工后改名"颐和园"。1900年八国联军侵入北京，慈禧太后出逃西安，颐和园再遭浩劫。1902年慈禧太后回到北京，下令立即修复颐和园，次年完工。

　　颐和园北依万寿山，南抱昆明湖，以佛香阁为主体，充分利用地形和水面，从假山的堆砌到曲径的走向，从楼阁的配置到花的点缀，从堤埂的修筑到亭桥的造型，充分继承和发扬了中国传统的造园技艺，表现出相得益彰的整体园林艺术效果，"虽由人造，宛自天成"，素有皇家园林博物馆之称。

　　The Summer Palace lies 15 kilometres northwest of Beijing Downtown area. It used to be an imperial garden and temporary palace during the Qing Dynasty (1644–1911).

　　Originally named Qingyiyuan, the Summer Palace was built in 1764. It has a total area of 290 hectares with a water surface of 220 hectares, and is divided into three scenic areas: one of the imperial court, one in front of the hill and one behind the hill. British and French soldiers invaded Beijing in 1860 and looted the Summer Palace. Many precious objects were taken away and buildings burnt down. In 1888 Empress Dowager Ci Xi rebuilt the imperial garden with 5 million taels of silver budgeted for the Imperial Navy. The reconstruction was completed in ten years. In 1900 soldiers of the Eight-Power Allied Forces invaded Beijing and looted the Summer Palace again. In 1902 Empress Dowager Ci Xi restored it in a year.

　　Longevity Hill rises on the northern shore of Kunming Lake. Foxiang (Buddha Fragrance) Tower dominates the hill. Scattered on the hill and around the lake are individual gardens, palatial halls and towers, painted corridors, bridges and a great variety of plants. The Summer Palace is the cream of Chinese traditional gardening art.

春到颐和园

Summer Palace in Spring.

▷

仁寿殿内景 其陈设如当年帝后临朝状。这里是中国近代史上变法维新运动的策划地之一。1898年光绪皇帝曾在此殿召见改良派领袖康有为,从而揭开了维新变法的序幕。后因封建保守势力反对,"百日维新"遂告失败。

Inside the Hall of Benevolence and Longevity The interior is kept as it was during the Qing Dynasty. In 1898 Emperor Guang Xu met Kang Youwei, leader of the reformists, in this hall and appointed him a high-ranking court minister. But the reform failed in 100 days because the conservative force was too strong.

东宫门 为颐和园正门,门为三明两暗的庑殿式建筑,中间正门供帝后出入,称"御路",两边门洞供王公大臣出入,其他人等从南北两侧边门出入。匾额"颐和园"三字为光绪皇帝御题。

East Gate It is the main entrance to the Summer Palace. The opening in the centre was for the emperor and the empress exclusively. The two side openings were for the use of princes and court officials. Eunuchs and soldiers used side gates to the south and north. The name plaque "Yiheyuan" in front of the gate was written by Emperor Guang Xu.

仁寿殿 是宫廷区的主要建筑之一,殿名寓示"施仁政者长寿"。此殿是清朝末年光绪皇帝和慈禧太后驻园期间听政的大殿。

Hall of Benevolence and Longevity (Renshoudian) One of the main buildings of the imperial court area was used by Empress Dowager Ci Xi and Emperor Guang Xu to give audiences.

大戏楼 位于仁寿殿西北德和园内。它建成于1895年,与故宫的畅音阁和河北省承德市清音阁同称清代三大戏楼,但以它为最大,且建筑精美,其势壮观。

Grand Opera Tower The imperial theatre in Dehe Garden was built in 1895. Three largest theatres were built by the Qing imperial court: one in the Imperial Palace and another in Chengde. This one in the Summer Palace is the largest.

慈禧太后画像 现存于德和园内。1905年,荷兰画家华士·胡博 (Hubert Vos) 应聘为慈禧太后画像,其时她已年届70,但画面形象仍风姿绰约,温文尔雅中透出皇权在握的威严。

Portrait of Empress Dowager Ci Xi The portrait was made by Dr·Hubert Vos of Holland when the dowager was already more than 70 years old. It is kept in Dehe Garden.

大清國慈禧皇太后
光緒乙巳年

万寿山前山风景区 以佛香阁和排云殿建筑为主体,其他各组点景建筑错落有致地分布于主体建筑的两侧和背后, 整体布局重点突出, 主宾分明, 既体现了皇家园林雍容磅礴的气势, 又不失婉约清丽的风姿。

Scenic Area in Front of Longevity Hill The main structures in this area are Foxiang Tower and Paiyun Hall. Many other buildings are arranged in neat patterns nearby. The area displays the grandness and magnificence of the royal family.

长廊 是中国现存廊建筑中最大,最负盛名的一座。它东起邀月门,西止石丈亭,中以排云门分为东西两段, 每段各伸出一截短廊连接对鸥舫和鱼藻轩两座临水建筑, 全长750多米, 共有273间画廊。

Long Corridor The 750-meter-long corridor runs from a Moon Gate in the east to Shizhang Pavilion in the west. All the 273 sections are painted with pictures either of ancient stories or landscapes. It is the longest and most famous corridor in China.

佛香阁 建于高 21 米的巨石台基上,它南对昆明湖,背靠智慧海佛殿,倚山而立,气势非凡。1860 年曾被英法联军烧毁,后照原样重建,是座宗教建筑。

Foxiang (Buddha Fragrance) **Tower** The tower stands on a 21-meter-high stone terrace on the sheer front side of Longevity Hill. It overlooks Kunming Lake in front and Zhihuihai Buddha Hall in the back. Other buildings stretch on either side of it in a neat symmetrical pattern. The tower was burnt down by British and French soldiers in 1860 and a new one was built on the site later.

排云殿 是万寿山前坡主体建筑之一，为慈禧太后诞辰祝寿而建。大殿横列复道与左右耳殿相连，共有房屋21间，均为朱柱黄瓦，甚是雄伟。

Paiyun (Dispersing Clouds) Hall One of the main buildings on Longevity Hill, it was specially built for Empress Dowager Ci Xi to receive her birthday greetings. Corridors link the main hall to side houses on both sides. Pillars in crimson colour and the roof with golden glazed tiles dazzle brightly in sunshine.

排云殿内景 内设九龙宝座，座旁有一对木雕大"寿"字，座前宝鼎成行，彩凤成双;殿内后间分立着一人多高的"麻姑献寿"人形。大殿陈设如此奢华，但每年仅在慈禧太后生日时使用一次。

Inside Paiyun Hall A throne carved with nine dragons is placed in the middle flanked by two carvings of the Chinese character for longevity. In front of the throne are bronze ceremonial pots, pairs of bronze phoenixes, and a life-size statue of Ma Gu presenting gifts. This extravagantly decorated hall was used only once a year on the birthday of Empress Dowager Ci Xi.

宝云阁　俗称铜亭。它铸造于
1755年，重207吨。亭为重檐
方顶，其菱花隔扇、柱、梁、斗
拱、椽、瓦以及九龙匾、对联
等均为铜质，整体呈蟹青冷古
铜色。它是世界上罕见的青铜
建筑精品。

Baoyun (Precious Cloud) **Tower**
Popularly known as the Copper
Pavilion, it was cast in 1755
with 207 tons of copper. The
square roof has several tiers of
eaves and latticed windows.
The pillars, rafters, rackets, tiles
and beams are all in imitation
of wood, giving a cold seasoned
lustre.

铜牛 位于昆明湖东岸。铜牛铸造于1755年。它两角耸立，双耳竖起，目光炯炯，形象逼真。牛背上铸有80个篆体铭文，说明它是用来镇水的。

Bronze Bull Cast in 1755, the bull has upturned horns and ears. Its eyes look intensively ahead. A note of 80 characters inscribed on its body tells that it was used to suppress flood.

◁
众香界 位于万寿山顶，是一座砖石结构的宗教牌坊，在牌坊的正、反面石额和智慧海的前后额上，刻着"众香界，祇树林；智慧海，吉祥云"，这三字偈语巧妙地把这里比作佛门福地。

Zhongxiangjie It is a Buddhist archway of bricks and stone on top of Longevity Hill. Inscriptions on it describe the place where it stands as a "Land of Happiness in the Buddhist World."

十七孔桥　昆明湖由湖堤划分为3个面积不等的水域，其中以十七孔桥所在的东水域面积最大。此桥东接湖东岸，西连南湖岛，全长150米，有如长虹卧波，蔚为壮观。

17-Arch Bridge　The 150-meter-long stone bridge links the South Islet with the eastern shore of Kunming Lake.

清晏舫 又名石舫，舫身系用巨石雕造而成，分上下层。取意"水能载舟，亦能覆舟"之意，喻意清王朝坚如磐石，水不能覆。

Qingyan Boat (Boat of Peace and Order) Alias Stone Boat (Shi Fang), the two-toried boat is carved from a huge rock. The name of the boat refers to the maxim that "water can support a boat and it can also overturn it," meaning the people could uphold a government and also overthrow it. The boat was used as a symbol of tight control of government of Qing Empire.

谐趣园　位于万寿山后山东麓，是颐和园的园中之园。它是仿江南寄畅园而建的，园内有5处轩堂，7座亭榭，百间游廊，5座小桥。所有建筑绕荷池展开，极富江南园林柔美清秀的特色。

Xiequ (Harmonious Interest) Garden Located on the eastern part of the back of Longevity Hill, the garden is an imitation of Jichang Garden in Wuxi City. It has five halls, seven pavilions, several corridors and five small bridges on a lotus pond. It is well known for the exquisiteness, typical to gardens south of the Yangtze River.

四大部洲　是万寿山后山的主体建筑。原建筑是藏式香严宗印之阁，象征佛教中的须弥山，1860年毁于战火，光绪年间重修时主殿改为佛殿，内供佛像。

Four Great lands　This main group of buildings on the back of Longevity Hill was devoted to Tibetan Buddhism. It was destroyed in 1860. When it was rebuilt in the reign of Emperor Guang Xu, the main hall was changed to worship the Buddha.

苏州街 位于颐和园后湖中段，街道蜿蜒曲折300多米，建筑面积3000多平方米。整个建筑以水当街，以岸作市，共有64座铺面，14座牌楼牌坊，8座小桥。

Suzhou Street The street runs 300 meters along the shore of Rear Lake behind Longevity Hill and covers an area of 3,000 square meters. There used to be 64 stores, 14 archways and eight bridges. The once busy commercial street has been restored as a tourist attraction in the Summer Palace.

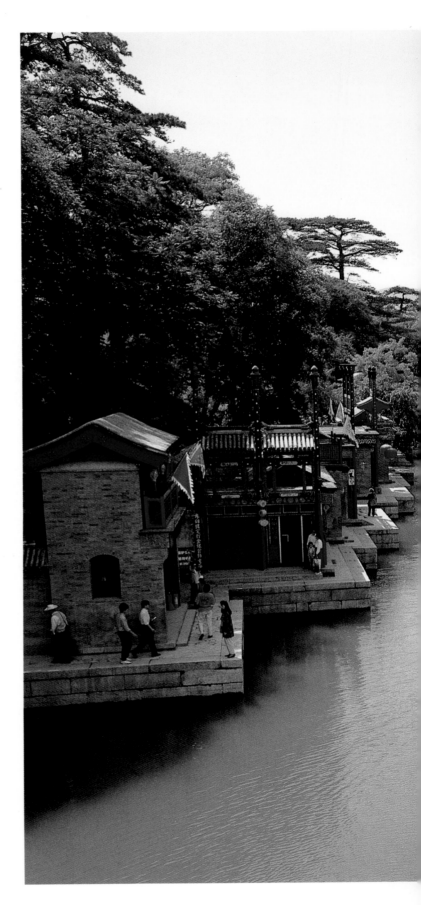

圆明园遗址公园

Yuanmingyuan (Old Summer Palace)

　　圆明园始建于1709年,经五代皇帝、历150年陆续建成;它由圆明、长春、绮春三园组成, 占地350公顷。园内集东、西风格胜景40处, 共有大型建筑145座。其中有中国传统的江南园林式建筑群, 有欧洲风格的宫廷区。它们或滨湖而建, 或傍水而立, 或掩映于绿荫, 或座落于山顶, 风格各异, 造型新颖, 极富诗情画意, 当年被人们誉为"万园之园"。

　　1860年和1900年, 英法联军和八国联军两度焚烧圆明园, 抢劫珍宝, 捣毁建筑, 使一代名园化为废墟。现在园林格局尚存, 经过整修, 少数景点已恢复, 大部分废墟遗址已被保护, 成为中外游客凭吊游览的风景区。

　　Construction of Yuanmingyuan, the Old Summer Palace, began in 1709 and continued for 150 years. The whole ground of 350 hectares was made up with three gardens: Yuanming (Round and Bright), Changchun (Everlasting Spring) and Yichun (Exquisite Spring). Forty scenic spots and 145 architectural objects followed both European and Chinese styles. There was an area built in imitation of an European palace. Painted pavilions, towers and corridors were seen along the shores of lakes, in trees or on hills. A stream flew through the three gardens. Yuanmingyuan was also the imperial museum with numerous precious articles, cultural relics and books.

　　But the marvellous man-made wonder was destroyed by British and French soldiers in 1860 and by soldiers of the Allied Forces of Eight Foreign Powers in 1900. It was only recently restored in part and has become a favourite tourist attraction in Beijing.

监碧亭 进圆明园南门，西行不远即为此亭；它座落于湖心孤岛上，须过桥登亭。它原是圆明园最大的方形亭，原亭已毁，图为修复的监碧亭。

Jianbi Pavilion Located on a small island in the centre of a lake not far from the front entrance to Yuanmingyuan, it can be reached only by boat. The original pavilion was destroyed a long time ago. It was rebuilt recently.

福海 为圆明园中最大的人工湖, 其中心有象征仙山的"蓬岛瑶台", 是帝王追求人间仙景的幻想境界。福海经修整, 已部分恢复原貌, 成为游人必至的休闲之海。

Sea of Blessings (Fu Hai) It is the largest artificial lake in Yuanmingyuan. In its centre there is an islet named "Jade Terrace" symbolising a deities' dwelling, the dreamland for rulers who coveted for immortality. After renovation the lake has partly restored to its former shape and become a good resort for visitors.

万花阵 实为西洋迷宫。在清代凡中秋之夜，宫女们头顶黄绸纱灯沿墙道穿行，皇帝则观赏流动的灯影，故又名〝黄花灯〞。原建筑毁于第二次鸦片战争，近年恢复。

10,000–Flower Formation (Wanhuazhen) It is a copy of a labyrinth of an imperial garden in Europe. During the Qing Dynasty in the middle of autumn the emperor would order court female servants to walk around in the formation with a silk lantern on each's head for him to enjoy. It was destroyed in 1860 in the second Opium War. The present formation is a recent reconstruction.

方外观 是一座清真寺，曾是乾隆皇帝的宠妃香妃（即容妃）做礼拜的地方。现仅存残基和部分石柱，以供后人凭吊。

Fangwai Temple It was a mosque built by Emperor Qian Long for his favourite concubine Xiang Fei who was a Moslem. Only a few stone pillars have been left from the looting in 1860.

谐奇趣 为西洋楼区最早的建筑物,其外观为中西合璧,颇具特色。当年为一音乐厅,专门演奏蒙、回民乐和西洋音乐。

Xieqiqu　The earliest structure in the European building group was a concert hall during the Qing Dynasty. Mongol, Hui and Western music was played in it. The exterior was a combination of European and Chinese styles.

大水法鸟瞰　这里是西洋楼区最宏丽的景观。大水法是由喷水池、壁龛式屏风和一对水塔组成的喷泉，中部水池有一组生动逼真的"十狗逐鹿"雕塑，当所有喷泉齐射时，声闻数公里。

Dashuifa It was composed of a fountain, a screen and two water towers, the most magnificent sight in the European area of Yuanmingyuan. When the "Ten Dogs Chasing a Deer", a group of sculptures in the fountain, spurted water, the sound could be heard several kilometres away.

远瀛观　是西洋楼区的中心建筑，曾作为香妃住所。残存的门柱雕刻精美，花纹生动。它似已成为圆明园遗址公园的标志，也是该园沧桑岁月的见证。

Yuanying Chamber　The Chamber in the middle of the European building group was a residence of Xiang Fei, a concubine of Emperor Qian Long. Carvings on the remnant gate pillars show the high level of ancient Chinese craftsmen.

◁

线法山　堆土成山，砖墙围护。山顶原有亭，循"之"字路登山入亭，可观西洋楼区全景。

Xianfa Hill　The man-made hill is surrounded by a wall. A zigzag flight of steps leads to the top where there used to be a pavilion from which one could have a good view of the European building group.

雍 和 宫
Yonghegong Lamasery

　　雍和宫位于北京东城区安定门内，是北京最大的喇嘛寺院。它建于清康熙三十三年（1694），原为雍正皇帝（1723—1735在位）即位前的府邸，称雍亲王府；雍亲王即帝位后将王府一半改为黄教上院，一半作为皇家游乐园。雍正三年改为今名。雍和宫由牌楼院、昭泰门、天王殿，雍和宫、永佑殿、法轮殿、万福阁等七进院落组成。院落由南至北逐渐缩小，而建筑物则渐次升高，这种"正殿高大而重院深藏"、"宫门向阳而层层掩护"的建筑格局，颇有聚龙窝凤的庄严气象。这正是中国传统的古建筑风格的完美体现。整个建筑巍峨壮丽，兼有汉、满、蒙、藏民族特色。

　　雍和宫藏有大量珍贵文物，其中五百罗汉山、金丝楠木佛龛和总高26米的白檀木大佛最负盛名，世称雍和宫木雕三绝。

　　The largest temple of Tibetan Buddhism in Beijing is located near Andingmen Gate in the northeastern part of downtown area. It was built in 1694 as the residence of Emperor Yong Zheng when he was crown prince. After he moved into the imperial palace in 1723 the new emperor turned half of his former residence into a lamaist temple of the Yellow Sect and the other half into a garden.

　　The whole ground of the temple is composed of seven courtyards divided by the Archway Compound, Zhaotai Gate, Hall of Heavenly Kings, Yonghe Palace, Yongyou Hall, Hall of the Law and Wanfu Tower. The courtyards become smaller from north to south while the buildings become higher. They are a perfect combination of central China, Manchu, Mongol and Tibetan architectural styles.

　　The lamasery keeps a great number of Buddhist statues and cultural relics. A jade carving of 500 arhats, a *nanmu* wood niche with gold thread and a 26-meter-high statue of Buddha are the best known treasures in the temple.

俯瞰雍和宫 它由殿堂楼阁、宝坊、角亭构成一组规模宏大的建筑，是北京保护最完整的喇嘛寺院。

A Bird's-eye View of Yonghegong Lamasery The many halls, towers, archways and corner pavilions form a majestic complex of buildings. It is the best preserved temple of Lamaism in Beijing.

牌楼院 由三座宝坊组成。1939年8月,侵占北京的日本军队用水泥梁柱偷换了宝坊的金丝楠木梁柱,将主要构件运回日本。图为被偷换梁柱的宝坊。

Archway Compound There used to be three archways of precious gold-eined *nanmu* wood. In August 1939 Japanese soldiers took the wooden pillars to Japan and replaced them with cement.

天王殿（雍和门） 为雍和宫的第一进大殿,原为雍亲王府的正门,改成喇嘛寺院后为庙的山门。门匾"雍和门"三字由乾隆皇帝用满、汉、蒙、藏四种文字题写。

Hall of Heavenly Kings (Yonghe Gate) The name plaque above the entrance to the hall, the first main hall and the front entrance to the temple, is in four languages of Han, Manchu, Mongolian and Tibetan in the handwriting of Emperor Qian Long.

布袋尊者　置于天王殿正中，中国民间俗称大肚弥勒佛。史载他为五代后梁（907-923）人，居浙江奉化。传说他常年手挽布袋，游历民间，见物即乞，将所得尽捐寺院，自称是未来弥勒佛转世。

Sage of Cloth Bag　Popularly known as Potted Belly Maitreya, a native of Fenghua in Zhejiang Province who lived during the Five Dynasties period (907-923). A story tells that he begged with a cloth bag and denoted all he got to Buddhist temples. He called himself reincarnation of the Future Buddha.

御碑亭　为方形重檐尖顶琉璃亭,建于公元1792年,内置高约6米的方形石碑,碑四面分别用满、汉、蒙、藏文书写喇嘛教的起源,为乾隆皇帝御笔。

Imperial Stelae Pavilion
The pavilion with a spire covered with glazed tiles was built in 1792. In it a six—meter high square stele has a record about the origin of the Lamaism inscribed by of Emperor Qian Long in Han, Manchu, Mongolian and Tibetan languages.

永佑殿内景 永佑殿原为雍亲王的寝宫,改为佛殿后内供三尊高2.35米的佛像,居中一尊头戴五佛冠、手托宝瓶的是无量寿佛,左为药师佛,右为狮吼佛。

Yongyou Hall It was originally the bedroom of Prince Yong. There are three 2.35-meter-high statues of Buddha in it. The one in the middle with a Five-Buddha crown and a precious bottle is Aparimitayus. On his left is Buddha of Medical Master and on his right is the "Lion Roaring" Buddha.

雍和宫 为面阔7间、前出廊后带厦的大殿,原是雍亲王接见文武官员的地方,改为喇嘛寺院后相当于大雄宝殿,内供铜质三世佛,即净琉璃世界药师佛、婆娑世界释迦牟尼佛、西方极乐世界阿弥陀佛。

Yonghegong Lamasery Originally it was the place where Prince Yong received officials. When the prince's mansion became a temple it was renovated to be the Daxiong Hall. Inside the hall there are bronze statues of Trikala Buddhas.

法轮殿 为前后出抱厦的大殿，其平面呈"十"字形。殿内正中供高6.1米的宗喀巴大师铜像。宗喀巴是格鲁教派的领袖，因此派戴黄帽、穿黄衣，所以又称黄教。图为法轮殿外景。

Falun Hall   The hall sits on a cross-shaped foundation. A 6.1-meter-high copper statue in the centre of the hall is of Tsongkhapa, founder of the Buddhist Yellow Sect. Followers of this sect wear yellow hats and robes.

法轮殿壁画　描绘于殿内东西山墙上，名为《释迦牟尼源流图》，共34段，详绘了佛祖从降生、学艺、出家、成佛和传教的过程。

Murals in Falun Hall　The 34 sections of wall painting in the hall depict Sakyamuni of his birth, study, becoming a monk and finally the Buddha in detail.

五百罗汉山 珍藏于法轮殿，山体用檀香木精雕而成，五百罗汉用金、银、铜、铁、锡五种金属制成，是一组艺术珍品。

500-Arhat Mount The carving is made of sandalwood while the 500 arhats of gold, silver, copper, iron and zinc.

万福阁 高25米,飞檐三重,斗拱交构,宏伟壮丽。万佛阁东西并肩排列着两座配楼,西为延绥阁,东为永康阁,二楼以飞廊与万福阁连成一体,峥嵘崔巍,有如琼楼仙阁。

Wanfu Tower　The wooden tower with multiple eaves is 25 meters high. Standing on either side of it are Yansui Tower to the west and Yongkang Tower to the east. The two side towers are connected with Wanfu Tower by corridors.

◁

迈达拉佛　耸立于万佛阁主殿,佛像通高26米,地上18米,地下8米,系用整棵白檀木雕凿而成。游人至此若看佛面,颇有仰目落冠之势。

Maidala Buddha　Maidala means Future Buddha in Mongolian language. The statue is 18 meters high, with eight meters underground. It is carved out of a whole piece of white sandalwood.

旃檀佛　供于万佛阁的东翼楼,为仿木铜铸佛像,其水纹衣饰、哈达均为铜质,却给人以柔软飘逸之感。佛龛和火焰背光系金丝楠木制成,共雕有99条蟠龙,大有群龙腾舞、呼之欲出的感觉。

Zhantan Buddha　The statue in the eastern wing tower next to Wanfu Tower is made of copper in imitation of wood. The ornaments on the clothes and silk *hada* ribbons are also of copper but appear like real cloth and silk. A niche and the flaming aura behind the Buddha's head are made of gold-veined *nanmu* wood. The 99 dragons look like to come out any time.

大 观 园
Grand-View Garden

　　大观园位于北京市西南郊，占地13万平方米，其中水面为2.6万平方米。园内有亭台楼阁、游廊水榭数百间，是一座典型的仿清代的官家园林。

　　大观园是北京市园林部门于80年代中期依据中国著名古典小说《红楼梦》描述的场景而建造的。《红楼梦》主要通过贾宝玉、林黛玉和薛宝钗三人间的爱情纠葛及其不幸结局，反映了18世纪中国封建贵族的兴衰。园内建筑采用中国古典建筑技法和传统的造园技艺，忠实于原著描绘的时代风尚，从山形水系的设计，庭院楼阁的建造以及室内陈设和人物雕塑，无不反映了那个特定时代的世风情俗。人们漫步园中，悠悠《红楼梦》古曲萦绕耳际，使人触景生情，怀古幽思油然而发。

　　Grand-View Garden is located in the southwestern part of Beijing. The garden has an area of 130,000 square meters with a water surface of 26,000 square meters. Following the style of imperial gardens of the Qing Dynasty it has several hundred houses, waterside pavilions and towers.

　　In the mid-1980s Beijing decided to build a garden according to the description of the Grand-View Garden in the classical novel *A Dream of Red Mansions*. The novel, through a love story between Jia Baoyu and the two girls of Lin Daiyu and Xue Baochai, tells the decline of an aristocratic family in the 18th century. The designers of the garden followed truthfully the customs of that time in the construction of buildings, the planting of trees and flowers and the making of statues of characters from the novel.

沁芳亭桥 建于园内中轴线，是诸小径咽喉要路，且四通八达，登亭四顾，园中景色尽收眼底。大观园的许多故事都发生在这里。

Fragrance—Seeping Pavilion Bridge The pavilion is situated on the central axis of the garden. All paths in the garden lead to the bridge. From the bridge one has a whole view of the garden. Many stories told in the novel *A Dream of Red Mansions* took place around the bridge.

怡红院　为小说男主人公贾宝玉的住所，这里粉墙环护，绿柳周垂，三间垂花门楼，四面抄手游廊；正殿五门抱厦，富丽堂皇。怡红院是金陵十二钗经常聚会，频繁活动的中心。图为怡红院垂花门楼。

Happy Red Courtyard It was the living quarter of Jia Baoyu. The main house has three ornamented doors. Corridors go around the wall in pink colour. It was the main gathering place of the 12 beauties in the novel. The picture shows its front entrance.

潇湘馆　是小说女主人公林黛玉的闺房。建筑以淡绿色为主调，屋前翠竹掩映，屋后荷叶田田，以此展示房主寄人篱下，内心悲苦而又孤高自许的性格特征。

Bamboo Lodge It is the living quarter of Lin Daiyu, the female main character in the novel. The house is dominated by the colour of green. In front of the house are bamboo stalks and behind the house there is a patch of field planted with lotus flowers. The environment is quiet but depressing to show the master's feelings as a sad girl living in other's house.

潇湘馆内景 黛玉与宝玉相爱,但他们双双蔑视功名利禄,不为封建家庭所容,有情人终不能成眷属。图中抚琴者为林黛玉塑像。

Inside Bamboo Lodge Lin Daiyu fell in love with her cousin Jia Baoyu. Both of them were rebellious against feudal conventions and their love was not approved by their elders. Lin Daiyu died of sadness after learning that Jia Baoyu had been deceived into marrying Xue Baochai.

◁

蘅芜苑　是小说另一主人公薛宝钗的住所。院内怪石嶙峋，青藤缠绕，仅留一曲径通向正殿前门，以展示这位大家闺秀表面温文尔雅,实则工于心计的性格特征。

Alpinia Park　It is the living quarter of Xue Baochai, another major character in the novel. The courtyard has many rockeries in strange shapes and plants. Only one path leads to the main house. The atmosphere shows the character of its master: externally docile and obedient and internally crafty.

省亲别墅　朝廷命官贾政的女儿贾元春为皇妃，别墅为元春省亲而建。主殿名为〝顾恩思义〞，大殿由前后两个院落组成，这里崇阁巍峨，玉栏绕砌，俨然皇家气派。

House of Reunion　The compound in the novel *A Dream of Red Mansions* was built for Imperial Consort Jia Yuanchun to stay when she returned home from the palace. The houses are high and surrounded with white marble balusters to display the extravagance of the royal family.

暖香坞 是小说中金陵十二钗之一惜春的住所。因这里比别处暖和,十冬腊月遮起门帘,仍觉温香拂面,正适合惜春作画,所以叫"暖香坞"。

Warm and Fragrant Cot It is the living quarter of Jia Xichun, one of the 12 beauties in the novel. Jia Xichun loved painting and liked the room very warm during winter.

稻香村 是金陵十二钗之一李纨的住处。这里有竹篱茅亭,果树稻田,水井酒幌;室内为纸窗竹榻,素椅木桌,一洗富贵气象。游人至此,感觉到的是山村野趣,田园风光。

Paddy — Sweet Cottage It is the living quarter of Li Wan, one of the 12 beauties in the novel. The courtyard is surrounded with a bamboo fence. Inside there are a thatched hut, rice paddies and fruit trees. A wine store banner hangs at the gate. The windows are covered with paper and the tables and chairs are of raw wood.

凹晶溪馆 建于园中低洼近水处,故名"凹溪",它与山脊上的凸碧山庄形成对景。这一上一下,一高一低,一山一水专为赏月而设。

Low Stream Studio (Aojingxi Studio) It is located at a low spot in the garden near water. The structure and Tubi (High Green) Villa on top of a hill make a good match. From the two spots one can have a good view of a bright moon.

滴翠亭 依照小说中"宝钗戏蝶"的故事而建的湖心亭，亭四面为游廊，一座曲桥接岸。登亭可闻水声，可观园景，亦可品茗抒情。

Dripping Emerald Pavilion The pavilion in the lake was where Xue Baochai played with butterflies in the novel. Corridors run around the pavilion and a bridge leads to the bank. People like to come here to hear the sound of flowing water over a cup of tea.

长　城
Great Wall

　　长城是中国古代的军事设施。它大约始建于公元前7至5世纪，那时各诸侯国根据自己的防御需要，分别修筑了数百公里乃至上千公里的长城。至秦始皇统一中国后，为防止北方匈奴奴隶主的南侵，于公元前214年命大将蒙恬和太子扶苏，率大军三十万和数十万民夫，历时10年，拆除中原各诸侯小国长城，同时把燕、赵、秦三国长城连接起来，并予以加固、扩充、延伸，完成了西起临洮，东至辽东，绵延万里的长城。此后，历代王朝都根据自己的防御需要对长城加以重修增补。

　　到了明代，前后修筑长城18次，历时200多年，使它西起甘肃省的嘉峪关，东至河北省的山海关，越群山，过草地，穿沙漠，横跨六省一市，总长达6700多公里，明长城大部分至今仍保存完好。北京八达岭、慕田峪、金山岭等处长城是明长城的代表。

　　The Great Wall was a gigantic defence work during ancient China. Separate walls were built in the 7th century B.C. by small warring states. After the unification of central China, Emperor Qin Shi Huang ordered in 214 B.C. to link up those walls in the north to prevent the *Xiongnu* (Huns) from coming to the south. The construction continued over 10 years. The Great Wall undertook 18 major repairs and extensions over 200 years during the Ming Dynasty (1368–1644). It runs 6,700 kilometres from Jiayuguan Pass in Gansu Province in the west to Shanhaiguan Pass in Hebei Province in the east over six province and Beijing and passes through high mountains, broad grasslands and immense deserts. Most of the Great Wall built during the Ming Dynasty has remained in good conditions.

　　The sections of the Great Wall at Badaling, Mutianyu and Jinshanling near Beijing are now famous tourist attractions.

八达岭长城 城墙高8.5米,顶宽5.7米,城上通道可五马并骑,十人并行。古人有"居庸之险不在关,而在八达岭"之说。

Great Wall at Badaling The section of the Great Wall at Badaling is 8.5 meters high and 5.7 meters wide on top. An old saying goes: "The strategic importance of Juyong is not the pass but the mountain of Badaling".

金山岭长城 因建于大小金山而得名。它位于北京市密云县和河北省滦平县交界处，是古北口长城的东段。古北口长城素为"京师锁钥"，是北京通往东北和内蒙古地区的三大关隘之一。

Great Wall at Jinshanling The section of the Great Wall at Jinshanling runs on top of Greater and Minor Jinshan Mountains along the border between Miyun County of Beijing and Luanxian County of Hebei Province. It is the eastern part of the Great Wall of Gubeikou, a strategic point safeguarding the capital and one of the three passes between the capital and Inner Mongolia.

居庸关 座落于燕山峡谷关沟中，有南北两口，水陆两关，自古为绝险关隘。由于这里地势险要，环境优美，远在金代（1115—1234）"居庸叠翠"就是燕京八景之一。

Juyong Pass A point of strategic importance on the road between Beijing and Inner Mongolia, it is located between two sheer mountains. "Piled Emerald at Juyong" was one of the Eight Grand Sights in Beijing as early as in the Jin Dynasty (1115—1234).

慕田峪长城 位于北京东北约70公里处。明洪武元年（1368）大将徐达筑边墙，自山海关抵慕田峪。此段长城以雄伟、险峻著称，加之自然环境优美，颇有高山园林的特色。

Great Wall at Mutianyu In 1368 General Xu Da of the Ming Dynasty built the Great Wall from Shanhaiguan to Mutianyu. The part in Mutianyu, 70 kilometres from Beijing, is well known for its dangerous terrain and beautiful surroundings.

牛犄角边 此段长城从东下山，至山腰又返回山顶，形似牛角，故名。

"Ox Horn" (Niujijiaobian) The part of the Great Wall runs down the mountain on the east and then turns up to the top, forming a bending like an ox's horn, hence the name.

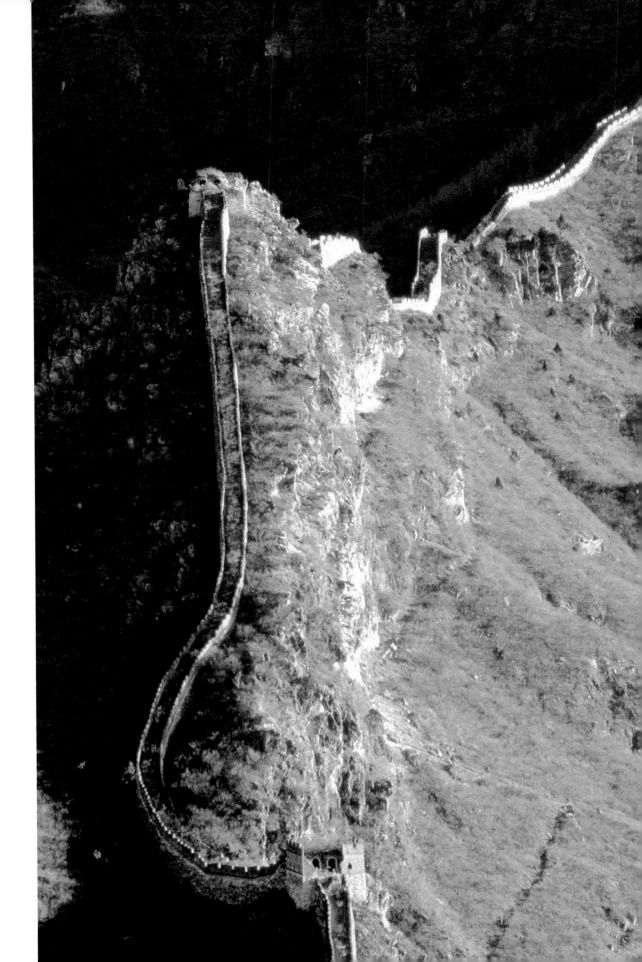

◁

大榛峪长城 位于北京怀柔县境内，距北京市区约80公里。此处地势陡峭，风景美丽。

Great Wall at Dazhenyu Located in the Huairou County 80 km from Beijing, the part is perilous and beautiful.

司马台关城 为明代所建，原关城已淹沉水中。此关西南不远处就是烟波浩渺的密云水库。图为司马台关城——二龙戏珠。

Simatai Fort Built during the Ming Dynasty, the fort had submerged in water long ago. Not far from it is the immense Miyun Reservoir. The picture shows "Two Dragons Playing with a Pearl" at Simatai.

司马台长城　西与金山岭长城相接，蜿蜒19公里，有敌楼35座。此段长城多建于峰巅危崖之上，险而又险；专家们称其为"奇妙的长城"。

Great Wall at Simatai　Adjoining to the Jinshanling section in the West, the 19-km section on top of towering peaks and cliffs has 35 watch towers.

天梯　为司马台长城的单面墙体，长约50米，呈直梯状沿山脊上升，陡峻险要。

"Heavenly ladder"　A 50-meter section of the Great Wall at Simatai runs on dangerous precipices.

明十三陵
Ming Tombs

　　明十三陵在北京昌平县境内,距城区约50多公里。陵区以长陵所在的天寿山为主峰,东、西、北三面群山环抱,构成一座大庭院,院门南开,蟒山、虎山雄峙两侧,恰似一龙一虎镇守大门。向南为开阔的盆地,温榆河从西北蜿蜒流来。中国封建社会后期明代自成祖朱棣(1403—1424在位)至思宗朱由检(1628—1644在位)等13位皇帝、23位皇后及众多妃嫔就埋在这群山环绕、松柏掩映的区域内,总面积约40多平方公里。

　　明十三陵从永乐七年(1409)始建长陵起,至崇祯十七年(1644)修建思陵止,历时225年,其工程之大,耗时之长,仅次于清代皇陵。在很长时间里,这片陵区一直披着一层神秘的外衣,不为世人了解。1956年,中国考古工作者成功地发掘了明万历皇帝(1573—1619在位)朱翊钧的陵寝—定陵,发现了地下宫殿,除棺椁外,出土金银珠宝、服饰玉器等宝物3000多件,揭开了定陵的秘密。1959年10月,建立了定陵博物馆,从此,明十三陵成为北京著名的旅游区。

The Ming Tombs are located 50 kilometres northwest of downtown Beijing. The burial ground of 13 emperors, 23 empresses and many imperial concubines of the Ming Dynasty (1368 – 1644) is embraced by mountains on three sides and opening to a flat basin on the south. Mangshan and Hushan mountains rise on either side. The Wenyu River flows to the northwest. The whole area of 40 square kilometres is covered with ancient pine and cypress trees.

Changling, the oldest mausoleum in the centre of the burial complex, was built in 1409 and Siling, the last mausoleum of the Ming Tombs, was built in 1644, 225 years after the first one. It was the most costly project with the longest time in the construction of imperial burial grounds in China. In those days the area with a circumference of several dozen kilometres was tightly guarded, giving it a mysterious atmosphere.

In 1956 Chinese archaeologists excavated Dingling, the tomb of Emperor Wanli (Zhu Yijun who was on the throne from 1573 to 1619) and unearthed 3,000 pieces of gold, silver, jade and precious stone in addition to the coffins of the emperor and his empresses. A museum was established at the site in October 1959. Since then the Ming Tombs have been a favourite tourist spot.

长陵鸟瞰 长陵是明十三陵的首陵，里面埋葬的是明代第三帝成祖朱棣（1403—1424在位）和他的皇后徐氏。明代各陵统称"宫"，陵由宫墙围括。长陵宫门内分别为棱恩门、棱恩殿、明楼和宝城；另有附属建筑如祠祭署、神宫监、神厨、宰牲亭等，俨然一座小皇宫。作为一种规制，其他各陵建筑与此大同小异。

A Bird's-eye View of Changling The oldest tomb of the 13 Ming Tombs contains the coffins of Zhu Di (reigned 1403–1424), the third emperor of the Ming Dynasty and his empress Xu. Originally there was a wall around the mound with a gate. The Ling'en Hall, Ming Tower, Precious City and some auxiliary establishment for sacrificial rituals and storage have remained. The construction of the Ming Tombs follows the layout of the Imperial Palace.

牌楼　是明十三陵的第一座建筑物，作为一种标志，意为陵区从此开始。牌楼建于1540年，为5间6柱11顶全石结构，牌坊和夹柱石雕刻精美，整体造型宏伟。

Stone Archway　The first structure a visitor sees at the Ming Tombs is a stone archway. Built in 1540, it has five sections, six pillars and 11 roofs.

长陵棱恩殿　是帝、后和遗官祭陵行礼的大殿，面阔9间，进深5间，寓意皇帝为九五之尊。此殿重檐垂脊，朱墙黄瓦，全木结构，为中国现存最大的楠木大殿。

Ling'en Hall of Changling　The main structure of the mausoleum was used by the living emperor and his empress to pay respect to the dead emperor buried in Changling. It stands on a three-tier white marble terrace and has a sloping roof with multiple eaves. This hall is the largest structure of *nanmu* wood still in existence from ancient times in China.

神路 为陵寝的引导之路。明十三陵神路长约10公里，它由石牌坊、大红门、大碑楼及36座石人、石兽组成，进入神路，给人一种庄严肃穆的感觉。

Divine Path Flanking the 10-kilometre-long path are 18 pairs of stone sculptures of human figures and animals.

棱恩殿内景 殿内外60根楠木大柱采自中国西南深山，居中四柱底部直径1.12米，两人不得围合，为世所罕见。

Inside the Ling'en Hall The hall is permeated with the scent from 60 *nanmu* pillars. A *nanmu* tree needed several years and cost many lives to be transported to Beijing from forests deep in the mountains in southwest China. The four pillars in the middle are 1.12 meters in diameter at the base.

定陵地宫入口 定陵是明代第十三位皇帝朱翊钧（1573—1620在位）和他的两位皇后孝端、孝靖的合葬陵。

Entrance to the Underground Palace Dingling is the tomb of Zhu Yijun, the 13th emperor of the Ming Dynasty (reigned 1573–1620) and his two empresses.

地宫甬道 是地宫通往各殿的走道。地宫是陵的主要部分，为全石拱券式无梁建筑，全长 87.34米，宽47.28米，由5个殿堂组成，总面积1195平方米。

Tunnel to the Underground Palace A tunnel leads to the burial chamber, called underground palace. The underground vault, entirely built with stone slabs without beams and pillars, is 87.34 meters long and 47.28 meters wide, comprises five halls and has an area of 1,195 square meters.

地宫中殿 殿内设置3座宝座，用来放置帝后牌位。雕龙扶手的是皇帝宝座，雕凤扶手的是皇后宝座。座前分别设有琉璃五供和一个青花云龙大瓷缸，缸中盛香油，并有灯芯，点燃发出黄光，谓之"长明灯"。

Central Hall of the Underground Palace   Memorial tablets of the emperor and his two empresses are placed on the three thrones. The throne for the emperor has handles carved with dragons and those for the empresses have handles carved with phoenixes. In front of each throne there is a huge porcelain jar which used to be filled with oil and a lit lamp-wick.

地宫后殿 为地宫主殿。正中设棺床，上置神宗和孝端、孝靖两皇后的梓宫。棺旁放26只盛满殉葬品的红漆木箱，周围散放玉料。棺床中央有方孔，内填黄土，称"金井"，是中国封建社会最高形式的葬礼。

Rear Hall of the Underground Palace   The rear hall contains three coffins for Emperor Zhu Yijun and his two empresses. Twenty-six lacquered boxes on either side of the coffins contain sacrificial objects. Jade and porcelain objects are placed around the coffins.

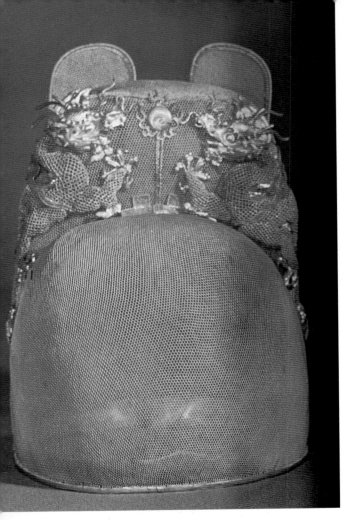

金冠 本名翼善冠，系明代帝王的常服冠戴，通高24厘米，用极细的金丝编织而成，上饰"二龙戏珠"，造型生动，制做精良，堪称国宝。

Gold Crown The 24-centimetre-high crown of the Ming emperors is woven with gold thread with close meshes and a smooth surface. The ornament on the top is of two dragons playing with a pearl.

凤冠 是皇后参加重大庆典时戴的礼服冠。冠上镶珠嵌玉，华贵异常。定陵共出土四顶凤冠，其中一顶饰珍珠3500多颗，嵌宝石150余块。图为三龙三凤冠。

Phoenix Crown Four such crowns were unearthed from Dingling. One of them is decorated with 3,500 pearls and 150 pieces of precious stones. In the picture is the "Three-Dragon Three-Phoenix Crown".

昭陵　为明代第十二位皇帝穆宗朱载垕 (1567—1572 在位) 的陵寝，孝懿、孝安、孝定3位皇后与其合葬。昭陵是十三陵中唯一被大规模修葺复原的陵墓。

Zhaoling　It is the tomb of Zhu Zaihou, 12th emperor of the Ming Dynasty who reigned from 1567 to 1572 and his three empresses. Zhaoling is the only one of the 13 Ming Tombs that has been totally restored.

思陵 是明朝末代皇帝思宗朱由检（1628—1644 在位）与周皇后的合葬陵。此陵原为田妃墓，故在十三陵中规模最小。思宗17岁即帝位，尽管励精图治，终因明朝已病入膏肓，无力回天。1644年，李自成率农民军攻入北京，思宗自缢煤山槐树下。

Siling It is the tomb of Zhu Youjian, the last emperor of the Ming Dynasty who reigned from 1628 to 1644 and his empress Zhou. It was originally built for Tian, an imperial concubine. Zhu Youjian ascended the throne at 17 and was diligent in his work. But the Ming Dynasty was so corrupt he could not save it. In 1644 the peasant uprising army led by Li Zicheng broke into Beijing. Zhu Youjian hanged himself at Meishan Hill behind the Imperial Palace.

编　　辑　宇　辰
责任编辑　元　素
翻　　译　宗　仁
摄　　影　高明义　姜景余
　　　　　宇　辰　张肇基
　　　　　胡维标　刘启俊
　　　　　何炳富　朱　力
装帧设计　宇　辰

Editors: Yuchen　Yuansu
Translated by: Zongren
Phtos by: Gao Mingyi　Jiang Jingyu
　　　　　Yu Chen　Zhang Zaoji
　　　　　Hu Weibiao　Liu Qijuen
　　　　　He Bingfu　Zhu Li
Designed by: Yuchen

图书在版编目（CIP）数据

北京风景名胜. 宇辰编; 宗仁译, -北京: 北京工艺美术出版社, 1999, 4

ISBN 7-80526-284-5

Ⅰ. 北京… Ⅱ. ①宇… ②宗… Ⅲ. 名胜古迹-简介-北京
Ⅳ. K928.701

中国版本图书馆 CIP 数据核字 (1999) 第 09094 号

北京风景名胜

*

宇 辰 编

宗 仁 译

北京工艺美术出版社出版

北京博诚印刷厂印刷

2000 年(16 开)第一版第二次印刷

ISBN 7-80526-284-5/J·117

05000